The Next Step: For Moderate To Advanced Equestrian Riders.

Short Stirrup to GRAND PRIX

Equestrian Centers
INTERNATIONAL

COACH MICHAEL

**Beijing 2008 Fundraiser for
US Pentathlon Stadium Jumping Team**

Dedicated to:

This book is dedicated to all of my students from 1966 through 2025, and to all my siblings who have put up with me throughout my professional equestrian years.
BUT! Especially to my sister, Denise Cintas—an outstanding rider, coach, instructor, and mentor to many—who has shaped so many incredible riders over the last 59 years, and to ALL THE WINNERS she has produced for national and international shows, both riders and horses!

CONTENTS

INTRODUCTION

LETTER FROM HAP HANSEN

Michael has had a lifelong passion for horses. His natural talent for riding and training horses and riders has earned many championships in the Hunter, Jumper and Equitation fields. His professional career began when his parents bought him Green Valley Acres in San Diego on his 18th birthday.

Prior to that he had traveled to the East coast to train with George Morris at the age of 16. He was awarded a scholarship from George Morris (One of the most prominent horsemen of our time). George Morris had set up this program to develop young talent from the West Coast. Michael Cintas studied under George for a year and then George Morris encouraged him to go back to California and start his professional career.

Michael Cintas has had a great career, not only developing top hunters, equitation and jumper horses and riders but he served as an Olympic Coach training the Men and Women's Pentathlon team for 5 Olympic Games.

I would recommend reading Michaels' books, as he is an interesting person with a wealth of knowledge in the world of horses and competition.

With respect...

HAP HANSEN

CHAPTER 1

OUR YOUNG RIDERS TODAY AND OUR FUTURE

OLYMPIANS TOMORROW

Matz at Pimlico

In the equestrian world, particularly in the art and practice of equitation—the discipline of horse riding and horsemanship—it is essential to have top instructors, just as seen in many countries worldwide. In any sport, an instructor or coach not only needs to have been a top athlete with a commendable background, but they also need to meet stringent qualifications if they decide to transition into coaching after retirement or injury. Becoming a coach, trainer, or chef d'équipe in equestrian sports—or any sport—requires meeting specific licensing standards.

Like in most countries, these standards typically include mandatory license renewals every five years. The renewal process involves rigorous evaluations, including written exams, verbal tests, and in-person demonstrations of skills. These assessments evaluate not only the instructor's technical expertise but also their presentation, demeanor, and ability to communicate effectively with students. During the verbal test, the national organization governing that specific sport ensures that the instructor can clearly articulate concepts, provide effective instruction, and foster understanding in their students.

In the United States, spanning nearly 250 years of history, we have seen some of the most naturally talented and unique coaches emerge. However, we have also encountered those who, despite their achievements, struggle to teach effectively due to poor communication skills. Recognizing this gap, I personally took Speech and Communication classes at UC San Diego's La Jolla campus to enhance my ability to articulate clearly, convey sensitivity, and maintain a demanding yet effective teaching style.

Unfortunately, many top equestrians, medal winners, and even past Olympians who transition into head coaching roles—whether at stables, riding schools, or training centers—often fail to improve their communication skills. While their knowledge and expertise are undeniable, their inability to effectively relay this knowledge to their students can hinder the athletes' development and progress.

Many top equestrians, regardless of their specific disciplines, often struggle with effective communication. While their knowledge and expertise are critical, their communication skills must be equally exceptional. A coach must deeply understand the diverse personalities of their athletes and recognize how each individual responds mentally and physically to coaching methods.

Unfortunately, many coaches teach from a singular mental perspective, often delivering their lessons in a flat, monotone manner. However, communication is far more dynamic—it has depth, variation, and intent. For instance, the difference between simply saying, "Listen," and emphasizing, "Hear me, and learn," illustrates the layered nature of effective teaching. Yet, in many cases, coaches fail to tailor their approach to the specific needs of the athlete, missing the mark in fostering true understanding and growth.

Communication is the cornerstone of successful coaching. A coach must go beyond knowledge transfer—they must embody the role of a teacher's teacher. This means not only articulating concepts clearly but also demonstrating them effectively. Just as in horse shows, a coach traveling with their students should occasionally ride and school the student's horse. By doing so, they provide a powerful visual aid, demonstrating techniques and strategies in action. This hands-on approach allows the student to see the potential of their horse and their own abilities, transforming the experience into a positive revelation. It instills confidence, helping the student recognize the exceptional partnership they share with their horse.

At any Training Center, a coach must ensure they are not teaching more than four students at once, regardless of the students' current riding level. This rule is essential for maintaining the quality of instruction and ensuring each student gets adequate attention. Personally, I never conduct group sessions with more than four individuals. Even in group lessons, my preference has always been one to two students at a time, as this allows for a more focused and effective teaching environment.

When considering a one-hour lesson, think about how much direct interaction and guidance each student truly receives from their coach. It's about ensuring that every minute is valuable and contributes to their learning experience. Over my 59 years as a professional and through operating five farms, I have always prioritized the needs of the students over sticking to the clock. Teaching should be about delivering what the student requires to progress and positively achieve the goals outlined for the session—not about rigidly watching the time. Remember, all aspects of teaching are relative to the student's progress and understanding.

The first lesson is critical in shaping a new rider's journey, and as a coach, you play a significant role in making it both positive and memorable. This is the moment to establish trust and respect while introducing your teaching style. Your demeanor matters immensely—present yourself with a happy and welcoming personality. The impression you leave will define your importance in the rider's initial experience and set the foundation for their growth and enthusiasm in riding.

CHAPTER 2

EDUCATION-EDUCATION-EDUCATION

Leslie Burr

As a beginner rider progresses from the first six months to their first full year of riding, it's time to explore new opportunities. At this stage, many beginner riders are ready to start horse showing. A well-educated and experienced instructor plays a crucial role in preparing students for this exciting next step. The instructor's role goes beyond just teaching the basics—they must inspire their students to become curious, engaged, and confident in their abilities.

The teacher should be fully qualified to guide the rider through this transition. For students interested in competing, the training will advance to include work on the flat, cavaletti exercises, small verticals, and offset oxers. Riders will also begin practicing jumping modified courses with 6 to 8 fences. These courses help novice riders refine their skills, combining techniques they've learned while developing their composure and building their memory and focus. This stage emphasizes the importance of flowing over fences in a confident, smooth, and rhythmic motion, instilling self-assurance along the way.

To ensure effective teaching, the instructor must have a solid background in both equitation and dressage, extending through at least the Third Level (yes, 3rd Level).

Additionally, the teacher should have a minimum of an "A" Show career background, demonstrating experience in Equitation Classes—both on the flat and over fences—as well as Hunter Classes and lower-level Dressage competitions up to the 2nd Level, with the ability to teach through the 4th Level, if not Prix St. George. Such qualifications ensure that the teacher is equipped to help novice riders—both children and adults—progress with proper instruction and effective communication.

Demonstrations are a key component of teaching at this level. Whether performed by the instructor themselves or a more experienced junior or adult rider, these demonstrations allow students to observe proper technique and execution in real-time, enhancing their understanding and application of the skills they are learning. A well-rounded and knowledgeable instructor ensures that each student receives the tools, guidance, and encouragement needed to thrive as they take this significant step in their riding journey.

It's time to get the Novice Rider paired with their first Horse or Pony. This exciting step involves careful coordination between the Teacher and the Head Coach, who may bring in potential mounts for the Novice Rider to try.

Alternatively, it is quite common for the Child and their parent(s) or the Adult Novice Rider to accompany their Head Coach and Teacher to various Farms, Equestrian Centers, or Riding Academies to explore and ride a selection of horses or ponies.

Throughout my career, I have consistently emphasized the importance of bringing any prospective sale horse or pony to my Equestrian Center for a one-week trial before finalizing any decisions. This approach ensures that the Novice Rider has ample time to become familiar with the horse or pony in their usual training environment, which is crucial for evaluating compatibility. In today's world, when purchasing your first show horse, this practice should be non-negotiable. It allows both the rider and the professionals overseeing the process to assess the prospect's suitability thoroughly.

If the trial week proceeds smoothly and the bond between the Student and the potential mount is evident, the next step is to arrange a veterinary examination. Typically, this vet check is conducted at the Equestrian Center, and the Head Coach will take care of all the necessary arrangements. Most riding and training facilities work closely with a trusted veterinarian who accommodates their clients and horses. However, if the purchaser prefers, they may opt to bring in an independent vet not affiliated with the Equestrian Center.

When purchasing your own show horse, the most critical guideline is to engage a veterinary clinic that specializes in show horses. A veterinarian with expertise in competition animals is invaluable in assessing the health and performance potential of the horse. For transparency and fairness, it is customary to use an independent veterinarian to represent both the Seller and the potential Buyer.

By following these steps, the process of finding and purchasing the right show horse becomes a structured, informed, and rewarding experience for everyone involved.

Your head trainer will guide you regarding the Sale Price and the final purchase price of the Show Horse. As part of the process, you are required to pay your trainer (acting as your representative) a Professional Finder's Fee, which typically ranges from 5% to 15%. This fee, referred to as the REP-Fee, compensates your trainer for their expertise and assistance. The owner of the Show Horse is responsible for paying the Seller and their representative directly.

For first-time buyers, it is crucial to familiarize yourself with the policies of the equestrian center you are dealing with. Ensure that both the Seller and the Buyer are fully informed of the actual sale price of the Horse. Unfortunately, there have been instances where individuals have added extra amounts to the Horse's sale price for their personal gain. This practice is highly unethical. As a buyer, it is essential to insist on a transparent and honest transaction. If your representative does not prioritize straightforward dealings, you are strongly encouraged to reconsider and walk away from the arrangement.

As the Buyer, you have the right to make an offer on the Horse you are interested in purchasing. However, this process should be guided by your head coach to ensure informed decisions. Additionally, your teacher and head coach are already aware of your budget, so any prospective horses you evaluate will fall within the price range you have specified.

CHAPTER 3

PURCHASING YOUR

FIRST SHOW HORSE

Kathy Kusner

When committing to purchasing a horse or any horse throughout your riding career, it is essential to consider several critical factors. Below is a detailed list of what you should assess and what both you and the Head Coach should look for during the process of trying out a new prospect:

1. **Attitude, Manners, and Demeanor**

   Pay close attention to the horse's overall attitude. Does the horse exhibit good manners and a calm demeanor? These traits can indicate how they will behave in various situations.

2. **Stall Behavior**

   Observe the horse in its stall. Look for signs of calmness and relaxation. Ears should be up, and the horse should appear alert but not agitated.

3. **Personality Around Other Horses**

   Evaluate how the horse interacts with others. Does it try to please, or does it show teasing or dominant behaviors? This insight can reveal its temperament and suitability for your goals.

4. **Changes in Personality During Work**

   Notice any shifts in the horse's behavior when being handled or ridden. A change, whether positive or negative, can reveal important aspects of its personality. A happy and cooperative horse is more likely to be a successful partner.

5. **Focus and Curiosity**

A horse that is curious but remains focused is ideal. This balance is a key indicator of its trainability and adaptability.

6. **Eating Habits**

Assess whether the horse eats seriously and consistently or if it is picky. Eating habits can impact the horse's health and performance.

7. **Ground Manners**

Examine the horse's behavior during grooming, cleaning hooves, brushing, and other basic care activities. Pay attention to how it handles mounting, dismounting, and the use of rub cloths on its face.

8. **Flatwork Skills**

Determine if the horse is well-balanced and educated in flatwork. A horse with solid foundational skills on the flat is easier to train for advanced tasks.

9. **Over-Fence Work**

Evaluate the horse's behavior and abilities when jumping. Is it brave yet steady, relaxed, and willing? Does it have a big stride and the ability to adjust when needed? Also, check for clean lead changes and overall confidence over fences.

10. **Voice Command Understanding**

Assess whether the horse responds appropriately to voice commands. This is an indicator of its previous training and ability to learn new skills.

11. **Trailer Loading and Travel**

Test how the horse loads into a trailer, handles travel (both short and long distances), and unloads. Smooth and cooperative behavior during these processes is crucial for future transport needs.

12. **Bad Habits**

Make detailed notes of any undesirable behaviors, such as cribbing, wind-sucking, or stall nervousness. Additionally, evaluate its tolerance for being blanketed, unblanketed, wearing a fly mask, and having boots applied or removed on all legs. Check how the horse handles trimming, mane pulling, and body clipping.

13. **Pre-Purchase Veterinary Examination**

Once a decision has been made to purchase, arrange for the horse to go on trial at the training center for a week. Immediately upon arrival, have your veterinarian conduct a drug test (blood test) to ensure the horse has not been administered substances that could affect its physical or mental state. Also, ask the vet to examine the horse's teeth to estimate its age if registration papers or a birth certificate are unavailable. Be aware that blood test results may take up to 72 hours.

14. **Tack and Equipment**

Avoid purchasing a horse ridden with a severe bit, heavy gadgets, or additional attachments beyond a standard bridle. These items may mask deeper behavioral or training issues. Look for a horse that competes and trains with minimal and appropriate tack.

Before purchasing your first horse, ensure you have developed a strong emotional and physical connection during your test rides. This relationship will determine whether you feel confident and secure with your potential new mount by the end of the trial period. Trust in your coach is essential—100% confidence in their guidance is non-negotiable, as their reputation is tied to the success of this decision. A top-tier coach will always prioritize finding the right horse that aligns with your needs and budget, ensuring the best outcome for you as a rider. Your first horse should possess the skill level and temperament of a seasoned School Master, often referred to as a "College Graduate," to provide you with a reliable and educational partnership.

Now, you're ready to have your veterinarian conduct a thorough pre-purchase examination. This process begins with a detailed physical evaluation of the horse, followed by flexion tests, which assess the basic soundness and mobility of all four legs. During the examination, the veterinarian will check all vital signs and run an additional blood panel to ensure the horse is in good health. After completing these initial steps, the veterinarian will proceed with a comprehensive set of X-rays. These X-rays will typically cover all four legs, focusing on key areas such as the ankles, hocks, knees, and stifles. In some cases, they may also include images of the back and neck to rule out potential issues.

If you are purchasing a show horse for training or competition, it's essential to budget for the complete veterinary evaluation. As of today's standards, the cost of this vetting process can range between $2,500 and $4,500.

In addition to veterinary expenses, you should account for the cost of the horse itself and any additional fees.

Typically, there is a representative fee of 12-15% of the purchase price that you would pay to your coach for overseeing the transaction and ensuring the horse meets your needs. These combined costs should be carefully considered to ensure a successful and informed purchase.

Training with your horse requires commitment and dedication, and it's essential to plan your approach thoroughly with your coach. This includes ensuring your coach continues to ride your horse, maintaining and building upon the education it already has, while also exploring opportunities for improvement. Together with your coach, the new owner will establish a detailed training and competition program, covering weekly and monthly schedules. These plans will also account for upcoming competitions to ensure you and your horse are prepared and progressing effectively.

The standard practices for training with your horse typically include the following:

A. **Structured Training Schedule:**
   You and your coach will collaborate to develop a comprehensive training schedule for your horse, with a minimum of three dedicated training sessions per week. On the non-training days, your role is

equally important. You'll visit the farm to flat your horse, take it on relaxed trail rides, and focus on meticulous grooming for both your horse and its equipment. This balanced approach keeps your horse in peak condition and fosters a deeper bond between you and your partner. Weekends are generally reserved for participation in local, county, or state-level horse shows, which offer valuable experience and test your progress.

B. **Active Participation is Non-Negotiable:**
Even if you are affiliated with an Equestrian Center that boasts top-tier staff and grooms who manage your horse and equipment with expertise, this does not excuse you from direct involvement. Owning and training a Horse is not just about showing up for rides; it's about taking full responsibility for every aspect of your horse's care and well-being. The equestrian world does not need riders who lack the heart, drive, and determination to put in the hard work. Your talent alone isn't enough—what matters is your willingness to give your all, with guts and glory, to ensure your horse thrives. If you're not ready to embrace this commitment wholeheartedly,

perhaps another hobby, like roller skating, would be more suitable for you.

C. **Be Early:** Arrive at your Equestrian Center at least 30 minutes before your session with your coach begins. This gives you ample time to prepare, focus, and mentally get into the right mindset. After your training, allow another 30 minutes to take care of your Horse's needs, such as grooming and equipment care. This time is essential for maintaining your Horse's comfort and well-being. Like any other sport, being an Equestrian requires complete commitment and discipline, and that includes giving your Horse the attention and care they deserve.

D. **Right Accessories are the Key:** Your saddle, the one you've been using with your new Horse, needs to be the right fit for both you and your Horse. If the saddle fits you well but isn't comfortable for your Horse, that can lead to problems for both of you. Always consult with your coach to make sure your saddle is a proper fit for your Horse. If necessary, you may need to invest in a new saddle that complements both you and your Horse's needs. Some popular saddle brands are The Pessoa,

Devocoux, and Hermes. Additionally, your Horse may require new tack such as a bridle, bit, or other equipment to ensure comfort and safety. Outfit your Horse just as you would outfit yourself with care and quality. Here are a few items to consider: a blanket, day sheet, cooler for after a bath, standing pillow wraps and bandages, tendon and ankle boots, and bell boots. Don't forget the fly mask with ears to protect your Horse from pests. Ensure you have a new leather and nylon halter with a lead rope and leather shank, as well as your complete grooming kit. Your Horse should live in a 12x12 box stall, and a 12x24 paddock attached to the stall is ideal for turnout. Horses thrive when given time to run, roll, and play, and having access to outdoor space is vital for their well-being. They also need their own time to relax, whether it's alone or with other horses nearby. Groom your Horse thoroughly, from head to toe, on a regular basis. You may bathe your Horse once a week with a bucket of warm water, body wash with liniment, and soap before competitions or travel to keep them clean and comfortable.

CHAPTER 4

YOUR TRAINING AND

TRAINING SCHEDULE

Beezie Madden

No Excuses—"NEVER" miss a lesson unless you are genuinely sick.

In the demanding world of Hunt Seat Equitation, Equitation Jumpers, and Medals, consistent training is non-negotiable. Success in this sport requires daily dedication, whether it's structured lessons with your coach or solo practice rides to refine your skills. With seven days in a week, you have six available for training—use them wisely.

At least one of those training days must include a dressage lesson with a knowledgeable and modern 21st-century dressage coach. Every Equitation Hunter-Jumper rider needs a solid foundation in dressage, both for their own development and for their horse's training. This discipline is essential in creating balance, control, and precision in the ring.

Additionally, once a week, you must incorporate a session called **"Comparable-Riding."** This involves training alongside another rider of a similar skill level and discipline, allowing both of you to observe, analyze, and learn from each other's techniques. During these sessions, your coach will facilitate a question-and-answer segment, providing real-time feedback and strategic insights. This structured approach will refine your riding skills and elevate your performance. Your coach and your horse will be your most valuable assets—treat them as such.

On weekends, you will be in the show ring. Many top-tier coaches across the country take their students to local competitions, ensuring they gain real-world experience. You will face challenges—the highs, the lows, and the unexpected obstacles that come with competing. Every moment in the ring, whether successful or disappointing, will shape your growth as a rider.

You will encounter setbacks. You will have moments of frustration. But every minor disappointment is a stepping stone toward major victories. Stay committed, set clear weekly and monthly goals, and track your progress relentlessly. By the end of your first year, you won't just be training—you'll be achieving. Write it down and make it real: **"MEET YOUR GOALS."**

When you and another future Show-Rider are in a lesson together, and your Coach asks you to critique the other Rider—whether on the flat, through gymnastics, or over a modified course—speak up. Clearly express what you observed, both visually and mentally. Identify what the Rider executed well and what adjustments could have been made to create a more polished, disciplined, and competitive ride. This is not just a casual exercise; it's an essential part of learning.

Likewise, be prepared to receive feedback from the other Rider. Critique is a valuable tool, not a personal attack. Use it to refine your skills, enhance your awareness, and develop a stronger understanding of correct form and technique. Remember, what you observe and feel is correct may differ from another perspective, making this exchange of insights crucial to improvement.

This teaching method is most effective when applied in a small group setting, ideally with no more than four Show-Riders in the ring. Mistakes happen—often without us realizing them. That's why this process is so important. No one becomes a top competitor overnight. Growth comes from consistent training, observation, and correction.

Work closely with your Coach and your Horse to develop your skills. Additionally, have a parent, friend, coach's assistant, or staff member record your rides, performances, and tests. Video footage is a powerful tool—it allows you to analyze your progress, spot areas for improvement, and track your development over time.

CHAPTER 5

"THE NATURAL FEEL"

(INSTINCT) YOUR POSITIONS!

McClain Ward

We focus on three key positions when riding to enhance balance and coordination: Cavaletti exercises, Cadence Poles, Gymnastics, and Modified Courses. These exercises refine the horse and rider's ability to maintain rhythm, stride length, and impulsion.

After completing the flat phase, your coach will introduce one or more of these exercises in the training arena, tailored to your current skill level.

Cavaletti Exercises

Cavaletti work involves setting poles at specific distances to develop stride control, rhythm, and balance. The poles can be spaced between **3'6" and 5' apart** depending on the desired trot stride—whether it's a collected rising trot or a lengthened stride. This exercise teaches both horse and rider how to maintain **consistent cadence, impulsion, and precise tempo** as they move through the varying distances. Transitioning from a **quiet 3'6" stride to a more extended 5' stride** reinforces **continuity of stride** and the ability to sustain tempo. Maintaining rhythm through these variations is key—riders should learn to "listen to the music and feel the rhythm" of their horse's movement.

Cadence Poles

Cadence poles are used at the canter to improve stride adjustment, balance, and coordination. The exercise begins with two poles spaced **6 feet apart**, creating a challenge where the rider must guide the horse through a smooth, controlled stride. By stepping in and out of the poles with proper front and back hoof placement, the horse develops greater awareness of its movement while maintaining balance. This exercise sharpens timing and stride control, helping the horse and rider refine their ability to adjust between the canter and gallop with precision.

A stride can range from 10 feet apart to 14 feet apart, categorized as a closed stride (shorter), a medium stride, or a lengthening stride (longer). These variations—10 feet, 12 feet, and 14 feet—are fundamental tools that will help you reach the Grand Prix ring. Understanding and controlling stride length is crucial, whether you're adjusting for technical courses or optimizing efficiency in a jump-off.

Additionally, we can work through the cadence poles using anywhere from one stride to seven strides. The distances between each stride should be measured accurately to ensure precision. These distances typically follow a pattern:

- **One stride**: 18 feet

- **Two strides**: 21 feet

- **Three strides**: 24 feet

- **Grand Prix standard**: 26 feet

When riding a line between two cadence poles, whether on the ground or slightly raised (which is preferred for better engagement), the goal is to maintain an accurate stride count. The ideal approach is to ride the line with the correct number of strides first, then add an extra stride the next time through, and finally leave out a stride to test adjustability.

Since a standard stride length is 12 feet, a seven-stride line would measure 84 feet. If you were to lengthen your horse's stride, you might extend that distance to 96 feet. Conversely, if you were galloping and needed to leave a stride out, the adjusted distance would still be 84 feet. This control over stride length is essential for both you and your horse's overall training program.

In competition, adaptability is key. **90% of all jump-offs are won by carefully leaving out strides and executing sharp, efficient turns.** To master this, you and your horse must develop versatility. Quick, balanced turns—where your horse moves like a spindletop—are just as critical as stride management.

All of these exercises should be practiced using both the **three-point** and **two-point positions** (now commonly referred to as the **half-seat**). It's vital to remember: **You follow, you do not lead.** The upper body should not dictate the movement—**it's always your SEAT and LEG that guide the horse.**

Your hands must follow naturally, moving from the elbow down, allowing for soft, elastic contact. **Commit to this technique.** A properly trained horse will stay on the bit because of the correct use of seat and leg, not because of rein pressure. The key to success lies in control, adaptability, and balance.

As I emphasized in my first book, dressage lessons are not optional when you reach the stage of performing technical work—they are essential. To develop both yourself and your horse into a complete and well-rounded team, you must commit to at least one weekly lesson with an experienced and successful dressage coach. Dressage is not just an isolated discipline; it enhances every aspect of your riding and solidifies the foundation needed to excel. By incorporating dressage into your training, you will refine your skills, improve your horse's balance and responsiveness, and ultimately become a more effective Equitation-Jumper rider. At the same time, your horse will develop into a stronger, more coordinated athlete capable of performing at higher levels.

However, be selective about who you train with. Many riders who have competed at the highest levels—both nationally and internationally—rank among the top 50 in the world. Their achievements are undeniable, but winning competitions does not necessarily mean they can teach effectively. Some of these top riders have mastered the sport through years of experience, yet they may lack the ability to break down techniques and explain them clearly. Riding skill and coaching ability do not always go hand in hand. When choosing an instructor, look for someone who not only possesses the technical expertise but also has the ability to communicate concepts in a way that helps you and your horse progress.

CHAPTER 6

"THE JUMPING CHUTE"

FREE-STYLE JUMPING

"Bellini" - 4 Year Old Thoroughbred
At Equestrian Centers International - Rancho Mirage, CA

Every horse or pony that is or will become a show horse or pony must learn to jump free-style. This training should always be conducted by a knowledgeable coach, with an assistant present in the chute to guide and support the horse. The coach will teach the horse to respond to voice commands, allowing the animal to learn how to jump independently. This method builds confidence and mental discipline, ensuring the horse remains focused while navigating different jump types, including verticals, oxers, triple bars, and combinations with varying distances. The jumping chute should never contain more than three jumps at a time, as additional obstacles can overwhelm and distract the horse.

When introducing a horse to the jumping chute, begin with a single low jump or ground poles. Once the horse gains confidence, gradually add up to three obstacles, incorporating a mix of verticals, oxers, and triple bars at increasing heights. During the first week, have the horse track left through the chute before switching to track right. Over time, the horse should become equally proficient on both tracks, ensuring balanced development.

Training in the jumping chute familiarizes the horse with different heights and distances, reinforcing their ability to adjust mid-air without a rider. Throughout the process, the horse will continue responding to the coach's voice commands, refining its technique and awareness. Many horses develop a strong sense of self-adjustment and body control, while naturally talented jumpers become highly focused and careful. As a result, the horse becomes physically adaptable and better prepared for jumping with a rider.

This training not only benefits the horse but also enhances the rider's experience. A well-trained horse, confident in its movements, makes over-fence riding feel seamless, creating a strong connection between horse and rider. Even experienced professionals continue learning and refining their skills, both in understanding their horses and improving their own techniques. The process of free-style jumping fosters adaptability, trust, and a greater sense of enjoyment for both horse and rider. And yes—horses are incredibly intelligent and thrive when given the opportunity to learn and grow.

Whenever your horses are working—whether you are in the saddle or handling them from the ground—they should always be equipped with front and back boots, along with a pair of Bell-Boots on their front hooves. This applies at all times to ensure their protection and well-being.

When training in the Dressage Court or riding across the Cross-Country Field, your horse should always be ridden in a Snaffle-type bit. Avoid using harsh or unnecessary equipment while you are still developing your riding skills. If your horse came with a more severe bit, it is likely because the previous owner or their trainers conditioned the horse to require it, often resulting in a complex or overly sensitive mouth. That is truly unfortunate.

There are many variations of snaffle bits available, but under no circumstances should you resort to a hard, heavy, or unnecessarily severe bit just to gain control over your horse. True horsemanship comes from learning to ride with soft hands, clear voice commands, and proper equitation skills. Mastering these fundamentals will provide you with better options for communicating with your horse, eliminating the need for more extreme measures.

Ensure that your veterinarian or an Equine Dental Technician properly floats your horse's teeth at least once a year. This is essential for their overall health and comfort.

Remember, your horse is just like a person and requires proper care!

For optimal health, all horses—including our show horses—should receive their vaccinations and deworming treatments four times a year, specifically in January, April, July, and October. Regular preventive care is crucial in maintaining your horse's well-being.

When participating in horse shows, be aware that event management may require additional vaccinations before allowing entry onto the show grounds. Across different regions of the United States, certain infections and diseases have been known to emerge. To ensure the safety of all competing horses, specialized vaccinations may be mandatory before participation. Failure to comply with these requirements may result in your horse being ineligible to compete.

Your Farrier (Very Important): There are thousands of horse shoers across the country, specializing in different breeds and hoof types. However, not all farriers are equally skilled. In the United States, about half of them are highly competent, 25% are adequate, and the remaining 25% lack the necessary qualifications to properly shoe a horse. Shoeing has always been an art, and it remains so today.

While it can be expensive, it is a crucial investment in your horse's overall well-being—especially its legs, haunches, shoulders, and back. Choosing the right farrier ensures that your horse is comfortable and protected, just as you would prioritize well-fitted, comfortable shoes for yourself.

A top professional farrier typically charges between $250 and $500 per session, with horses needing new shoes every 5 to 7 weeks. In our experience, we generally have our horses shod every 6 weeks.

Your Horse's Diet and Care: Just like people, every horse has a regular diet tailored to its needs. However, a show horse requires a specialized diet that includes additional supplements to support its performance as an equine athlete. The specific dietary requirements of your horse should be carefully discussed with your trainer, veterinarian, feed and nutrition supplier, and coach. Several factors influence their diet, including the level of competition, age, conformation, and any existing anatomical concerns.

For horses competing in equitation, hunter, jumper, and dressage disciplines, routine joint care is essential. Hock, stifle, and ankle injections should be administered once or twice a year, depending on whether your horse follows a heavy, medium, or light competition schedule. Proper maintenance helps ensure their longevity and ability to perform at their best.

Rest and recovery are just as important as training and competition. Horses, like humans, need time off to recharge. For at least one to two months each year, a show horse should step away from the demands of competition and simply be a horse—allowing them the opportunity to relax, move freely, and rediscover their natural instincts.

Your Groom! **"The Real Master of Horse Care"**: A groom at any equestrian establishment is worth their weight in gold, silver, and platinum. For years, they have been casually referred to as stable boys or stable hands— but they are far more than that. They are the backbone of every horse facility, the key that unlocks every stall, paddock, and in-and-out at barns across the country.

Equestrian grooms play an essential role in the care of hunters, jumpers, dressage horses, ponies, and Grand Prix performers. They are the unseen force ensuring that horses receive the highest level of attention and care. While the head coach and their staff are responsible for developing both horse and rider, the groom is the foundation that makes it all possible. Without them, no equestrian facility could function.

These dedicated professionals are the first ones in the barn each morning and the last to leave at night. They feed the horses, clean the stalls, turn them out for play, and carefully lunge them in either bitting rigs or natural settings. They ensure that every horse is in peak condition, not just through daily routines but by maintaining their overall well-being.

Grooming a horse isn't just about running a brush over their body and legs—it is a full-scale art form, a meticulous process that requires patience, skill, and a deep understanding of each horse's needs. From the first touch to the final polish, every step matters. The work of a groom is not just a job—it is a commitment, a craft, and a passion that keeps the equestrian world moving forward.

A daily routine begins with each horse being led into the wash-rack or grooming stall the moment they leave their stall or stall-and-paddock setup—what we refer to as their apartment. This is the first step in their daily preparation, ensuring they are clean, comfortable, and ready for the day's work.

The groom has a dedicated grooming compartment, fully stocked with all the necessary tools and products to bring out the horse's best external appearance. Inside the grooming box, every item serves a purpose—from brushes and combs to hoof picks, coat polish, and conditioning sprays—ensuring that each horse is meticulously groomed and perfectly turned out. A thorough grooming session takes about 15 to 20 minutes, during which the groom carefully cleans, smooths, and polishes every inch of the horse, preparing them to look and feel their best.

After the rider has completed their lesson or show class, the groom takes over once again. At least 30 minutes before the horse is returned to its apartment, the groom begins the post-ride care, which includes cooling down, washing, and checking for any signs of stress or injury. Every detail is attended to, from wiping down the tack to ensuring the horse is comfortable and content.

Despite their skill and dedication, grooms have rarely received the level of appreciation and respect they have earned and truly deserve. They are not just caretakers; they are masters of their trade. A top groom commands a salary between $2,500 and $5,000 per month, in addition to housing and often a food allowance. Their work never truly stops—every moment is spent refining, perfecting, and enhancing the horse's beauty, as if preparing them for the most prestigious presentation. A top groom's horse should always look as if it belongs in a stunning oil painting— elegant, flawless, and breathtaking.

Clients are consistently informed that tipping their horses' grooms should be done on a weekly or monthly basis—never daily, as that would be excessive. On average, a top groom typically receives between $50 and $100 per week per horse/rider in tips. The only person who acts as an intermediary between the groom and the trainer is the barn manager, making this individual the second most critical member of the team.

It is not uncommon for well-established show stables to attempt to recruit top grooms from competing training centers. In some cases, the level of competition for skilled grooms has become so intense that grooms frequently switch barns, even changing colors to align with a new training center. At the core of it all, clients should recognize the value of their grooms—expressing gratitude, respect, and appreciation as they would for family.

Modern show training facilities operate like structured businesses, with dedicated staff handling various responsibilities, including secretarial and bookkeeping tasks. In the past, the trainer or barn manager often juggled multiple roles—acting as the secretary, bookkeeper, head trainer, and barn manager simultaneously. However, the equestrian industry has evolved into a professionalized operation where every staff member has a defined role and reports solely to the barn manager.

CHAPTER 7

"ON THE ROAD"

George Morris

**"Impeccable Position" and the true Equitation "The 2-Point"
Position (Now per Coach Michael, is referenced as the 'HALF-
SEAT-POSITION')**

From Short Stirrup to Grand Prix! You've outgrown your starting point, moved beyond the familiar farm, and are now stepping into serious horse shopping with your trainer and the farm members you ride with. Together, you form a team—a close-knit group we'll refer to as "TEAM-MEMBERS," representing not just yourselves but also your barn, trainer, and staff.

At a top barn, a Road Manager travels with the Head Trainer, staff, and show riders to every competition and shopping trip, ensuring everything runs smoothly. Your groom plays a crucial role in your overall show experience. Just as you present yourself in your best show outfit, your horse must be impeccably turned out—well-groomed, with spotless tack—reflecting the care and professionalism of your team.

Now it's time to compete—whether you're stepping into the Short Stirrup division for the first time or preparing for the Gran-Prix. Every Gran-Prix rider once started in the lower levels, learning the fundamentals, refining their skills, and understanding what true competition means. No one skips the process, and no one starts at the top.

If you're feeling nervous, that's completely normal. In fact, it's a good thing. We call it "Nervous Energy," and it's something every rider experiences, from beginners to seasoned professionals. That surge of adrenaline can sharpen your focus and fuel your performance. I've always reminded my students, no matter their age or division, that nerves aren't something to fear. With time, discipline, and experience, those nerves transform into confidence—and, eventually, into blue ribbons.

For riders competing in Jumpers and Equitation classes over fences, walking the course with your coach is a crucial step. It's a major advantage that allows you to break down each element of the course before stepping into the ring. Together with your trainer, you'll plan your approaches to the jumps, analyze the best turns to take, determine the angles for slicing fences, and decide when to ask for your horse's gallop. Every detail matters, and the more prepared you are, the more in control you'll feel when it's time to ride.

When the Rider and Trainer walk the Course, they analyze the layout, which typically consists of 10, 12, or 15 obstacles. These obstacles may include combinations, where two or three consecutive jumps set one or two strides apart are counted as a single jumping effort. Walking the Course allows them to determine the optimal number of strides to take between fences, strategize for the Jumpoff, and decide when it might be necessary to leave out a stride in a line for a more efficient ride.

To qualify for the Jumpoff, the rider and horse must complete the first round within the designated time while ensuring that all obstacles remain intact. This means no knocked-down rails, no refusals, and a ride completed within the allowed time—a clean, smooth performance.

Beyond personal achievement, every successful round is the result of collective effort. Your horse, your coach, your fellow riders, your barn manager, and your groom(s) have all contributed to the moment. Each class you compete in is an opportunity to learn and grow, making every round a new experience.

As you gain more experience in Horse Showing, you will notice a shift in your mindset. The excitement of competing will begin to outweigh any initial nerves, and you will naturally develop the attitude and determination of a true competitor—a "WINNER." With each event, your confidence will grow, and the competition atmosphere will feel more familiar and enjoyable.

After you and your Horse return home to the Equestrian Center alongside your Coach, Friends, and Staff, the focus will shift to rest and recovery. You will take a well-earned day off, and your Horse will do the same—possibly even two days, depending on the intensity of the event. Once it's time to ease back into your routine, you will return to the farm and prioritize your Horse's well-being. This means allowing them time to relax with turn-outs, baths, and grazing, ensuring they have the chance to recover fully. From there, you will gradually resume light work, incorporating flat work exercises and a couple of trail rides to maintain conditioning without overexertion. This short period of downtime and tranquility is essential for both you and your Horse, providing the necessary balance between competition and recovery.

Back to the Drawing Board

Let this be understood and accepted—once an athlete or equestrian (both Horse and Rider) is in the making, the journey of Training, Education, and the pursuit of Equestrian Knowledge never truly ends. There is not a single National or International Coach who has ever closed the BOOK and convinced themselves that they have mastered it all. That will never happen.

Being an equestrian athlete—just as your Horse is— means that daily learning is a necessity, not an option. Every day presents an opportunity to refine skills, correct mistakes, and apply the knowledge gained from previous experiences. Success in equestrian sports is not just about individual effort but about the continuous partnership between Horse and Rider. The reality is simple: "Both of you will always be in training." Whether through groundwork, riding drills, or competition reviews, learning is ongoing. The more you invest in your education and training, the stronger your bond and performance will be, ensuring you remain competitive as a team.

After every competition, your first training session becomes a critical step in your development. You and your Coach will analyze video footage of your performance, breaking down the moments where you and your Horse excelled and identifying areas that need improvement. Your Coach will highlight inconsistencies—both technical and strategic—so that you understand what worked and what didn't. More importantly, the discussion will focus on how to adjust, correct, and prevent those issues from resurfacing in future competitions. This process is not about criticism but about refinement, ensuring that each lesson builds on the last, shaping you and your Horse into a more synchronized and competitive team.

Your next riding session with your coach will focus on either ground poles or small obstacles, depending on what best suits your training needs. During this session, your coach will recreate the challenges you faced in your last ride to help you understand and correct them. For example, if you struggled with turns between obstacles, late lead changes, or maintaining rhythm, these elements will be addressed specifically, as they directly impact your overall time on the clock.

You'll work on executing the correct strides, whether on a straight path, a bending line, or a long gallop of more than six strides leading into the second obstacle. Additionally, your session will reinforce the feel and control needed when holding your horse off a vertical, riding down to the base of an oxer, or navigating a double or triple combination without getting trapped. These exercises are essential and will be incorporated into your first jumping lesson to ensure consistency and improvement.

Typically, after your last competition, your horse would not be jumped for four to five days, except for light cavaletti gymnastics if necessary. This refresher session serves as a crucial part of your post-competition adjustments, allowing you to make corrections while the experience is still fresh in your mind.

We are here to keep you informed about your Jumper Style Equitation journey, including County, State, and National Medal Classes. These crucial classes serve as the foundation for riders aspiring to become skilled Equitation Jumper Riders. The Equitation and Medal Classes play a vital role in shaping future Grand Prix competitors, teaching them the essential elements of style, finesse, and technique necessary to excel in both National and International competitions.

Each of these competitive events demands a deep understanding of Style, Feel, Finesse, and above all, 100% Commitment. A truly dedicated Young Rider or Adult must recognize the importance of developing into an Outstanding Equitation Rider. This journey requires cultivating an extraordinary level of awareness—often described as a "sixth sense"—starting from their early years as a Junior Rider.

The foundation for success is built early, typically between the ages of 5 and 6, when riders first begin their equestrian education. From the very first lesson, students learn the fundamentals of "Riding Right," establishing correct posture, balance, and control. Equitation is not just about riding—it is about mastering body position, communication with the horse, and developing an instinctive connection between rider and mount.

In their introductory sessions, New Students are immediately introduced to the significance of body language in riding. They begin to understand how their posture, balance, and subtle cues influence the horse's movements. From the start, they are taught to both mentally and physically connect with their horse, developing an awareness of its size, strength, and power.

A Proper Teacher ensures that learning is not an intimidating experience but an exciting and enjoyable one. Riders will feel inspired, motivated, and eager to develop their skills, laying the groundwork for a lifelong passion for equitation.

Becoming an exceptional Equitation Rider opens the door to competing in the Jumper Ring and can ultimately lead to representing your country on the international stage, including the Olympics. Developing a strong foundation in equitation is essential for long-term success in the sport.

I have absolutely no objection to a young rider starting their journey with a few initial lessons on a retired show pony or horse. However, I strongly believe that a young rider should not remain on a pony for an extended period. Once their legs are long and strong enough to make effective contact with a more suitable mount—ideally a horse between 15 and 15.2 hands—then all their training should be conducted on horses, not ponies.

To reach the highest level as a Young Equitation Rider or to develop into a confident and capable adult rider, proper training and appropriate mounts are key. Young riders must continue refining their skills through every stage of growth, while adults must focus on mastering their form from the very beginning. Your hands, seat, and legs should work in harmony to create a polished and elegant riding style.

Stay committed to maintaining peak physical condition. Keep your diet balanced, get adequate rest, and always maintain perfect posture. With dedication and discipline, you are on your way to achieving excellence in equitation.

CHAPTER 8

EXERCISES ON THE FLAT AND

VARIABLE OBSTACLES, "VERSATILITY"

WITH HORSE AND RIDER!

Ashlee Bond

"ON THE FLAT" – Always Mount From The Ground!

Lazy legs make a lazy rider! Unless you're injured—like I am, being an amputee of my left leg. Even then, I still mount from the ground by lengthening my stirrup leather. Once I'm in the saddle, I adjust my leather back to the correct length, aligning it with my ankle bone. No delays. No hesitation. I immediately move into my 3-point position, preparing to warm up my Horse on my own.

We begin walking forward. My body is physically relaxed, my mind fully engaged. As we move, I shift seamlessly between my three riding positions: first, the stable 3-point position, then into my 2-point, and finally stretching straight up into my 1-point position—as if I were seven feet tall. This constant transition keeps me balanced, aware, and connected with my Horse. I repeat this sequence at least a dozen times, walking on both tracks, ensuring my body and my Horse are in sync. These exercises take about 5-7 minutes, enough time to establish rhythm and focus.

Then, I return to the track on the left, picking up a rising trot. This helps loosen both my Horse and me. As we move into the trot, I continue with my 1-2-3 point exercises, crossing my diagonal to work both tracks, always staying in tune with my Horse's movement. I focus on relaxing every part of my body, from head to toe. When the moment feels right, I let the trot naturally transition into a canter, maintaining my three body positions throughout.

This structured yet fluid warm-up takes about 10-12 minutes. By the end, both my Horse and I are fully prepared—physically and mentally—to dive into our flatwork and whatever new challenges the day brings.

Walk, Trot, Canter, Gallop—often referred to as a Hand-Gallop—and then back down to a walk. Once both tracks have been used, it's time to work on Collective Measures and achieving a Semi-Natural Feel.

Collection is not just about pulling the reins—it's about mastering the coordination between your legs, seat, and hands. You apply leg pressure into your hands while maintaining a deep, balanced seat. This means sitting firmly on your seat bones, never on your tailbone, and keeping your crotch positioned over the pommel of the saddle. No one—man or woman—should be hitting high notes from discomfort or bruising their inner thighs.

Your hands should be positioned approximately 2–3 inches above the withers and spaced 3–4 inches apart. The goal is always to maintain a straight line from your elbow to your hand and from the rein to the snaffle bit. Collection isn't about restricting movement; it's about driving the horse forward from its hindquarters. When done correctly, you'll feel a powerful spring from the hind end as the energy moves through the horse's back, up through the shoulder, and into its head and neck. This is when your horse will accept the bit, allowing you to achieve true collection.

You work on Collective Measures at all gaits: the walk, sitting trot, posting trot, and canter. When collecting your horse, the key is to be forgiving—you don't pull on the mouth. Instead, you push the horse forward using your seat and legs, allowing the movement to come from behind. Riders with educated hands understand that force is never the answer. This is why having a skilled coach is critical; they will guide you toward proper collection rather than artificial restraint.

Whether you're riding a collected walk, trot, canter, or hand-gallop, softness is key. When your horse is correctly collected and soft in your hands, reward them. A simple pat on the neck goes a long way, but more importantly, you should slide both hands forward for 2–3 strides, signaling to the horse that their effort was correct. This release is a reward—it lets them know they're doing it right.

Too often, I've seen trainers and riders hanging onto young horses' mouths, creating a false sense of leverage. This is not collection. Bracing your back and forcing a horse into a frame is not the same as developing true balance and softness. A horse should accept the rider's hands willingly— not be forced into submission. Always strive for true connection, not control.

Simple Gymnastic Exercises for the Horse and Rider

Start with bounce exercises using raised cavaletti set approximately 6-12 inches off the ground. This foundational exercise helps both you and your horse develop balance, coordination, and rhythm as you train together.

Begin with two raised cavaletti, spaced 10 feet apart. Approach at a collected canter, ensuring your horse maintains a steady rhythm. As you reach the first cavaletti, give a small cluck and use a short stick (bat, crop) to bridge your reins in one hand, applying a quick, light tap behind your leg if needed. This encourages your horse to remain engaged and responsive. The first time your horse understands and reacts correctly, you establish a critical foundation for communication.

Repeat this exercise 5-6 times, ensuring consistency and confidence in your horse's movement. Work on both the left and right rein to develop even strength and balance. Just like riders, horses have a natural preference for one side—whether left or right-handed—so training on both tracks ensures ambidexterity for both of you.

On the following day, add a third and possibly a fourth cavaletti to the exercise. Repeat the same process 5-6 times on each rein, gradually reinforcing your horse's ability to navigate the sequence smoothly. As you and your horse progress, you will be able to increase the height of the cavaletti and continue refining your gymnastic work.

Your top coach will provide technical guidance throughout this process, ensuring proper execution and development as you advance in your training.

The following exercise is called the WINDMILL. To set it up, place four poles on the ground in a windmill pattern, positioned at 12 o'clock, 9 o'clock, 6 o'clock, and 3 o'clock. You will ride on two tracks—one following the 3-6-9-12 o'clock sequence and the other along the 12-3-6-9 o'clock sequence. The center points of all four poles should be set 10 feet apart.

The goal is to execute this exercise smoothly and in sync with your horse while maintaining a steady canter. Your horse should be bending correctly on whichever track you're riding, from its head through the shoulders, neck, and body. Maintaining focus is key—for both you and your horse—to execute the windmill pattern effectively.

Before progressing to the canter phase, start by trotting through the center point in both directions. This helps establish control and balance before moving into the more advanced work. When you begin the canter exercise, note that there are no extra strides in between the poles—each movement is a bounce. This forces both horse and rider to be precise while maintaining impulsion, balance in turns, and rollbacks.

As you and your horse become more confident and coordinated, the four Cavaletti poles will be gradually raised—starting from 6 inches off the ground and increasing to 12 inches. This progression will further refine your horse's agility, balance, and responsiveness, making the exercise both effective and efficient.

Our next exercise involves setting up four jump poles through the center of the ring. These poles should be positioned so they are centered between the two short sides of the arena. Use 12-foot jump poles, each accompanied by a single upright standard on either side of the ground jump pole.

Start by placing the first jump pole on the ground eight feet from the middle of the short side of the arena. Then, set the next jump pole 15 feet ahead of the first one, following the same setup—each with a standard on both sides. Continue this pattern until all four poles are placed, maintaining consistent spacing. Since most rings are at least 200 feet long, there will be ample room to complete the exercise correctly.

To begin, you will trot into the exercise and focus on executing a serpentine pattern with four equal loops. This requires precise control, as you must start and finish at the designated reference point. Once you complete the exercise on a left-hand track, you will repeat it from the opposite side of the ring, now tracking right.

As the rider develops a clear understanding of the pattern, guided by their coach's expertise, the ground poles will gradually be converted into small vertical jumps starting at 3 inches. With time, practice, and progression, these jumps will be raised, eventually reaching heights of up to 3 feet 6 inches.

As both horse and rider become more familiar with the exercise, the four obstacles will be adjusted to include a mix of verticals and oxers. The sequence will progress from a ground pole to jumps at 2'3", 2'6", 2'9", and finally 3 feet. Throughout the exercise, the coach will guide the rider on coordinating their turning radius and executing smooth lead changes.

This is fundamentally a "look and see" exercise, where the horse and rider must communicate through precise body language. Mastering this drill will not only refine balance and rhythm but also strengthen the connection between horse and rider—an essential skill for advancing to Grand Prix-level combinations.

Your Body Language at the Walk, Trot, and Canter: Both Horse and Rider

When riding, both the horse and rider operate within the center of their equilibrium. Every movement, whether a turn, transition, or lead change, requires subtle shifts in the rider's balance and position to guide the horse effectively.

Turning and Positioning

When making a left turn—whether it's a simple turn, a half-turn, or a full circle—the rider should shift slightly toward the right center of their equilibrium. This shift is accompanied by placing the outside (right) leg slightly behind the girth while maintaining more weight on the right seat bone. The rider's right hip engages, transferring balance down through the right calf and into the heel. Additionally, the right foot should turn slightly outward, helping to support the turn. Once the turn is completed, the rider re-centers themselves back into equilibrium.

The same principles apply when making a right turn, but in reverse. The rider shifts their weight toward the left center of their equilibrium, moves their outside (left) leg slightly behind the girth, and applies more weight through the left seat bone, hip, and leg. The left foot should turn slightly outward to maintain balance and control through the movement. Once the turn is completed, the rider returns to a centered position.

Lead Changes and Track Alignment

Once the rider gains confidence navigating obstacles, such as a four-loop serpentine, lead changes should become smoother and naturally align with the intended track. As the rider transitions through the loops, they should step into the opposite hip bone from the inside of the turn. At the same time, the outside leg shifts slightly behind the girth, while the opposite inside hand applies indirect rein pressure with a few additional ounces of weight. This coordination ensures that upon landing after the obstacle, the horse is on the correct lead for the next track.

Maintaining awareness of these subtle shifts in body language allows for clearer communication between horse and rider, promoting balance, precision, and fluid movement through each transition.

**Hampton Classic Friday
Chris Kappler**

CHAPTER 9

"PLANNING YOUR WEEK

WITH YOUR COACH"

Diane Grod

You and your coach will collaborate to develop a system that works best for both you and your horse. Below are structured training suggestions to enhance your horse's performance and your riding skills:

1. **Freestyle Jumping Chute (Once a Week)** – This exercise allows your horse to build confidence, develop rhythm, and improve jumping technique without the rider's influence.

2. **Rest Day with Turn-Out (Once a Week)** – Your horse should have one full day off each week, including at least one hour of turn-out. This provides mental and physical recovery while maintaining movement to prevent stiffness.

3. **Trail Ride (Once a Week)** – A 45-minute to one-hour trail ride with your horse fully equipped (Tenson, ankle, and bell boots) helps with relaxation, endurance, and exposure to different terrain, which benefits overall balance and adaptability.

4. **Structured Lessons (Four Days a Week)** – Your training schedule should include one dressage lesson and three equitation lessons covering flatwork, gymnastics, and over-fences.

- **Dressage Lesson (Once a Week)** – This session refines your equitation position and enhances your understanding of proper mounting and foundational flatwork techniques. Every jumper and equitation rider should incorporate flatwork through at least the second level of dressage. This improves agility, balance, and overall control.

- **Equitation Lessons (Three Times a Week)** – These sessions focus on technical elements, including precision in flatwork, gymnastic exercises for coordination, and over-fences practice to refine jumping skills.

By consistently integrating dressage into your routine, you strengthen your horse's agility and responsiveness, which translates to improved performance in jumper and equitation competitions. This structured approach ensures that both rider and horse develop the necessary skills to compete effectively.

The horse and rider should be able to smoothly and effortlessly adjust stride length at any gait, whether shortening, collecting, or lengthening. The rider should be able to execute shoulder-in and half-pass movements in both directions within sequences of six, eight, or ten strides on both tracks. Lead changes should be performed in threes and fours with precision. The pair should also be capable of transitioning from a full gallop to a halt and executing walk, trot, and canter transitions within a controlled three-stride tempo. Additionally, the rider should be able to canter directly from a standstill, back up three to four steps, and immediately transition into a gallop.

The canter stride should be consistently adjustable, shortening and lengthening every three, four, or five strides to develop balance and responsiveness. When cantering across the diagonal of a 180-200 foot ring or court, lead changes should occur every three strides to maintain rhythm and engagement. This level of control and adjustability encourages the horse to develop scope, agility, and confidence in their movements. If the horse possesses the necessary athleticism and training, they will become a careful and efficient jumper within their competitive division, positioning both horse and rider as a winning team.

An excellent exercise to further develop these skills is to incorporate cross-country training. Under proper supervision, take the horse into large open fields, gallop across varied terrain, and jump a few fences while relying on your eye for distance and timing. This type of work builds trust and strengthens the partnership between horse and rider, creating a deeper level of compatibility and confidence.

LEARNING TO RIDE OFF YOUR EYE, LEARNING TO COUNT STRIDES

Your Coach will guide you through this process, but understanding how to adapt as a rider will make it easier and more intuitive. With practice, you will develop the ability to approach a fence and accurately judge your distance 5, 6, or even 7 strides away.

This skill is built on three key elements: Rhythm, Feel, and Motion.

Understanding Rhythm

To ride effectively, you must first learn the natural rhythm of the canter and gallop. The canter is a three-beat gait, but instead of counting "1-2-3," you will focus on a smooth **one-and-two** cadence. This helps establish a consistent, balanced rhythm.

Stride Length and Adjustability

Your Coach will teach you how to canter on different stride lengths:

- **10-foot stride** (a more collected canter)

- **12-foot stride** (a standard working canter)

- **14-foot stride** (a lengthened stride, allowing for greater ground coverage)

Mastering these variations will give you the control needed to adjust your horse's stride length based on the type of jump or course you're riding.

Pole Exercises for Accuracy

To develop your eye and stride control, you will start with two ground poles. Your Coach will set them at different distances across the width of the arena, helping you practice adjusting your horse's stride while maintaining a steady rhythm.

Later, as you progress, the gallop will come into play. The gallop is an extension of the canter, where stride length increases along with speed (measured in miles per hour). But for now, the focus is on refining your ability to judge distances and count strides accurately.

By practicing these foundational elements, you'll gain the confidence and skill to approach jumps with precision and control.

Set up two poles 24 feet apart. You will canter down the track, ensuring you complete the exercise on both leads to work in both directions. In the next set, increase the distance between the poles to 36 feet, which will require two strides between them. The third set will be spaced 48 feet apart, allowing for three twelve-foot strides in between. Finally, the fourth set will be placed 60 feet apart, where you will take four strides in between.

As you go through the exercise, count your strides out loud—not just in your head. Hearing your own voice keeps your mind engaged and helps maintain focus. Your sound is also an important cue for both you and your Horse.

During this training process, your coach will have you add an extra stride in each set and then remove one. This means you will need to adjust your Horse's stride within the standard 12-foot length. To do this, maintain a vertical alignment in your position, and fit two shorter strides into the space while keeping your Horse moving with uphill elevation and sustained impulsion.

Your coach will continue to vary the distances so that you can work on adjusting your cadence between 10, 12, and 14-foot strides. To develop an accurate eye, always count your strides aloud during training sessions. Your coach will remind you periodically to reinforce this habit.

Here's a hypothetical question to challenge your understanding of stride length and rhythm. Ask yourself this and answer for both yourself and your horse.

Question: You are in the main arena at your equestrian center with your coach. The arena is 240 feet long. Your coach instructs you to begin cantering on the short middle side of the arena, tracking left. From there, you will canter up the long side while maintaining a steady, consistent 12-foot stride. The question is:

"How many strides will you complete on the straightaway before reaching the short side?"

Answer quickly: **18 strides, 22 strides, or 20 strides?**

Remember, you are maintaining a **12-foot working canter** with steady rhythm, feel, and motion. The answer is provided in the following section.

The most effective way to complete this exercise is to **look up and focus beyond your last obstacle or your next**

objective. Keep your rhythm consistent, feel your horse beneath you, and maintain smooth forward motion. Your awareness should extend to your horse's entire body—**in front of you, under you, and behind you.** This exercise should be practiced in both directions to develop balance and precision.

The Importance of Counting Strides

Mastering stride counting requires dedicated practice across multiple disciplines. As you prepare for competition, both mentally and physically, you and your coach will **walk the jumper or equitation course at least twice** to familiarize yourselves with the distances. If any distances raise questions, you may walk the course a third time to ensure clarity.

In the **first round** of your jumper or equitation class, you will ride the course as designed, ensuring that each distance is executed as intended. However, in the **jump-off**, your strategy will change. Since you are riding against the clock, you will naturally **leave out a stride** where it makes sense. This means shifting from a **12-foot stride in the first round to a 14-foot jump-off stride** on long approaches. When leaving out strides, you do so in lines of four or more strides—but **never in a combination.**

It is crucial to understand that removing a stride in a **1-2 stride combination** is unfair to the horse. Physically, the horse is already giving maximum effort, and mentally, it can lead to stress and confusion. The only exception is if you are riding a **well-schooled horse (never a young horse)** that is trained to make tight rollback turns immediately after landing, based on balance and adjustability. A skilled rider can influence stride shortening when approaching a double or triple combination, a bending or broken line, or a related distance.

This concept will be explored further as we advance to **larger combinations and complex courses** designed by professional course designers. These exercises will build upon your understanding of stride management and competitive riding strategies.

(Answer to the Question: 20 Strides.)

CHAPTER 10

"RIDING MILES IN THE SADDLE"

Rodney Jenkins

We quickly learned just how many hours we would need to dedicate to the saddle. There were no shortcuts, no easy paths—just time, effort, and commitment. If you're serious about this journey, I strongly encourage you to stick to your schedule, remain disciplined, and, if you are a Junior, ensure your parents are fully engaged in the process. Every ride matters. You and your horse should always enter the training arena prepared—physically, mentally, and emotionally—so that every session is productive.

Even the best coaches occasionally seek another professional's opinion. No one is a "know-it-all," no matter how much experience they have. Riding is a lifelong pursuit of learning, refinement, and growth. Many of our international riders have made us proud, not only with their exceptional performances in competition but also with their deep respect for their horses, their composure under pressure, and their ability to make intelligent corrections when their horses misbehave—always followed by genuine affection and respect.

The greatest riders of our time have shared common traits—sensitivity, patience, intellect, and talent. They fell in love with every horse they rode and treated each one as a partner. Discipline was at the core of their success. Their names are etched into the history of the sport, and we hold them in the highest regard. Some of the most respected international competitors and coaches, including many Olympians, include Ian Millar, Conrad Homfeld, Chris Kapler, Hap Hansen, Joe Fargis, Will Simpson, Richard Spooner, Susie Hutchison, Katie Monahan, Rodney Jenkins, Dianne Grod, Ashlee Bond, George Morris, Jimmy Kohn, McLain Ward, Beezie Madden, Bill Steinkraus, Kathy Kusner, Leslie Burr, and Michael Matz, to name just a few.

These remarkable individuals have exemplified talent, humility, and an unwavering love for their horses. Beyond their personal achievements, they have dedicated themselves to helping others, passing on their knowledge, and mentoring the next generation of riders. Their success wasn't just measured in wins but in the way they carried themselves—as riders, as coaches, and as human beings.

Every ride had to be their best. Every lesson they taught was an exercise in clear communication, deep knowledge, and positive reinforcement. They never sought just to win— they aimed to create better riders, better horsemen, and better horses. Every new horse they trained was given every opportunity to reach its full potential, both mentally and physically. That is the legacy they built, and it is the standard we should all strive to uphold.

To reach your full potential, you need to be at a show barn—an equestrian center that specializes in equitation and jumpers at the highest level. This means a barn that is structured and aligned with your coach to focus on competitive success. These programs are designed specifically to prepare riders and horses for competition, attending a range of horse shows, from schooling events to local, county, and national-level competitions.

As you develop your skills in the jumper ring, you should also compete in as many equitation and medal classes as possible during each show. This well-rounded approach will prepare both you and your horse—mentally, physically, and competitively. The key is to accumulate as much experience as possible, consistently building your knowledge and refining your abilities.

When it comes to training and correcting your horse, always operate with a mindset of "Reward and Correction" rather than punishment. Your horse must associate training with clear guidance, not fear or frustration.

Competing at a high level in the show ring requires a full-time commitment. If you are unable to dedicate yourself fully, that's completely fine. However, in that case, it's important to recognize the difference between riding for fun and pursuing competition seriously. If your goal is simply to enjoy owning and riding your horse without the demands of a competitive program, a boarding stable would be a more suitable environment. This ensures that your horse's potential is not wasted, and your coach's time is spent on riders who are fully committed to the sport.

Choosing a Sport That Brings You and Your Horse Together

Committing to a sport with your horse is not just a hobby—it's a partnership, a relationship, and, in many ways, a marriage. You need to ask yourself a crucial question: "Can I fully dedicate myself to this sport, knowing it requires my complete commitment?" This commitment extends beyond riding. It includes the countless hours spent on groundwork, care, and building trust with your horse. If you find that your schedule conflicts with training, adjust the conflict, not the training. Emergencies are exceptions, but outside of that, your training time must remain sacred. 100% commitment—no excuses.

As emphasized earlier in this book, keeping a journal is essential. Document everything—what you learned that day, what you corrected, what needs improvement, and your short-term and long-term goals. This journal will be more than just notes; it will serve as a roadmap for your progress, helping you stay accountable and focused.

Parents, Children, Teenagers, and Adults: Understanding Financial Costs, Growing Pains, and Commitment

No matter your role—Junior, Amateur, Parent, or Financial Provider—commitment is required from all parties.

For a Junior Rider (under 18), owning and competing with a show horse is not just about having the title of a competitor. If you own a competition horse, you must actively train and compete. If you are serious about riding, understand that your education is now twofold: your academic schooling and your education as a competitive equestrian. Before your parents or financial provider invest in this demanding and expensive sport, you must first prove that you are fully committed to it.

This means making yourself available every single day after school or, if your coach allows, before school (as I personally did). A minimum of five days a week is non-negotiable. Without this level of dedication, you are not truly in this sport.

For an Amateur Rider (18 and older), the sport is often a lifelong pursuit, with many continuing to ride into their 60s and even 70s. The same principles apply—consistency, financial responsibility, and a commitment to both training and competition.

No matter your level, remember this: equestrian sports demand unwavering dedication. If you want to succeed, commit fully.

Junior and amateur riders typically commit to an extended period of training and competition. A solid 30% of junior riders, even after heading off to college, continue riding and showing throughout their academic years. However, it is common for parents to advise their son or daughter that once college begins, it will be time to step away from horse showing and focus entirely on their studies.

Until that point, maintaining a strong commitment is essential if you aim to become a highly competitive show rider. Regardless of whether you have the financial means to support your riding without limitations or work hard to afford the sport, careful budgeting is still necessary. Unexpected expenses will always arise.

For instance, you will inevitably spend money at tack shop vendors at horse shows. Your farrier will be another ongoing expense—your horse may throw a shoe or require specific shoeing for jumping on grass. Additionally, you may need the services of the horse show veterinarian for an unexpected health concern. Every aspect of the sport comes with costs, and understanding these financial commitments is crucial for riders and their families.

To ensure financial preparedness, here is a list of expenses to review. Whether you are an amateur, a junior rider, or a parent, discussing these costs with your coach— or whoever they designate—is an important step in managing the financial side of competitive riding.

The List!

Here's a detailed list of the expenses involved in competing with your horse:

- **Round-Trip Transportation for Your Horse** – Ensuring safe and reliable transport to and from the show.

- **Pre-Paid Stabling Fees** – Covering the cost of your horse's stall for the duration of the event.

- **Entry Fees & Show Expenses** – Includes all necessary competition fees, association dues, and any additional charges required to participate in the show.

- **Golf Cart Rental** – Providing convenient transportation around the showgrounds.

- **Day-Care Fees for Your Horse** – Covers the care and maintenance of your horse on show days, ensuring they are properly fed, groomed, and attended to while you are at the event.

- **Trainer & Staff Fees** – Daily training and coaching services from your trainer, along with compensation for any supporting staff assisting with your horse's care.

- **Hotel, Meals, and Travel** – Accommodations and travel expenses for you, your trainer, and staff. Depending on the location, travel may include airfare.

- **Split Fees** – Shared costs for services such as tack stalls, setup, and additional equipment.

- **Feed & Shavings** – Providing the necessary nutrition and bedding for your horse while at the event.

- **Grooming Stalls & Grooms** – Ensuring your horse is properly cared for, including grooming and stall maintenance.

- **Tips for Grooms, Vet, and Farrier (if needed)** – Additional gratuities for those involved in your horse's well-being during the show.

- **Tack Store Purchases** – Any last-minute supplies, replacement gear, or equipment needed while at the venue.

- **Monthly Home Board & Training Fees** – Your regular boarding and training costs remain ongoing, even while competing.

- **Competition Schedule** – Expect to compete at least twice a month. Local shows tend to be more cost-effective, while out-of-town events come with additional expenses.

By understanding these costs in advance, the financial planner can budget effectively, allowing the rider and their horse to focus entirely on training and performance without financial distractions.

Jimmy Kohn

CHAPTER 11

"SITTING DOWN WITH YOUR COACH AT THE DRAWING BOARD"

EXAMPLES: YOUR REALITY IS BEING TESTED!

THEN OFF TO YOUR HORSE SHOW!

Katie Prudent

Here are two possible scenarios for a jumping class:

Scenario 1: One Meter (3'3") Jumper Class, Table 2-B

In this class, you will navigate a course consisting of 10 efforts, including a one-stride, a two-stride combination, and one roll-back. The objective is to complete the Course cleanly and within the time allowed. If you accomplish this, ensure you have plenty of space to gallop through the timers at the finish—this will position you to win when the bell signals the start of the jump-off.

From the moment you enter the ring, commit to a strong, balanced gallop. Ride with precision and confidence, making decisive turns and maintaining a steady rhythm. Your hand-gallop should reflect the trust and connection between you and your horse. Approach each jump with focus, ensuring you clear every obstacle cleanly. Keep your mindset sharp—testing yourself in each round is key to improving your performance.

Remember, the entire Course is your challenge, and every detail counts. After the Class, take the time to review your performance with your coach. Analyze your ride, your horse's response, and your decision-making throughout the Course. This reflection will help strengthen your skills and refine your approach for the next competition.

Corrections:

Here were the key issues that need to be addressed:

1. **One-Stride Combination Error:** You had a stop in your one-stride combination, specifically between the vertical and the oxer. This happened because you lost momentum and didn't fully commit to the stride. Your hesitation translated to the Horse, causing a break in the flow.

2. **Leaning Out Between Fences:** Between the two fences, you leaned outward, which shifted your weight onto the Horse's neck and shoulder. This imbalance made it more difficult for the Horse to maintain a straight and steady approach. Remember, your Horse is sensitive to even the smallest shifts in balance, and your position directly influences his movement.

How to Fix It:

- **Upon Landing:** Stretch up into your three-point position immediately. This helps maintain balance and control.

- **Ribcage & Hands:** Lift your ribcage to stay upright and centered. Keep your hands 2-3 inches above the withers and 2-3 inches apart to provide steady contact without restricting movement.

- **Lower Body Support:** Sink into your heels to anchor yourself in the saddle. Closing your leg will keep your Horse engaged and forward-moving.

- **Focus & Commitment:** Keep your eyes up and commit to the one-stride transition. As you approach the oxer, focus on looking above the back pole—this will help you ride through the jump smoothly.

- **Be One with Your Horse:** Your Horse relies on your confidence and position. Ride with purpose, maintain balance, and move as one with him through the entire combination.

Equitation Over Fences 3'3" – A One-Meter Class:

This class consists of eight fences, including a one-stride combination and a trot fence, totaling ten efforts. Your coach will go over the entire course with you, breaking down each section to identify areas for improvement and assessing the overall quality of your ride. The goal is to refine your technique, correct mistakes, and enhance your understanding of the course.

One of the key aspects of your training will be recognizing mistakes and learning how to correct them. For example, if you canter the last stride before a trot fence due to tension, instead of maintaining a steady trot, your coach will explain why this happens and how to fix it. The correction might involve using a calm verbal "whoa" rather than reacting with abrupt rein pressure. Keeping your patience, maintaining steady breathing, and staying composed will help prevent anticipation and allow you to execute the movement correctly.

These discussions with your coach will be invaluable. You will bring your journal to each session, noting both the mistakes and their solutions. Writing down a negative experience and turning it into a positive learning opportunity will reinforce your progress.

Mistakes are a natural part of your development as a rider. By analyzing and addressing them immediately after your class, you will significantly reduce the chances of repeating them. Over time, this process of learning and refining your skills will set the foundation for greater success, ultimately preparing you for the Grand Prix ring.

Entries for the horse shows you are competing in will be handled by your coach and road manager, except for local shows. They will submit your entries, along with those of the other show riders, at least two weeks before the start of the competition. Each day, you will have a clear schedule of the classes you are competing in. However, there may be instances when your coach decides to scratch one of your classes or make a substitution, either for a lower or higher-level class, based on strategic adjustments or unforeseen circumstances.

One to two weeks before the competition, you are expected to review the USEF Rule Book thoroughly. This serves as your primary reference, providing detailed explanations of the rules and requirements for each of your classes. It is essential that you fully understand these guidelines, as they outline the expectations, qualifications, and specific regulations for your events. Before heading to the show, you should go over any uncertainties with your coach to ensure complete clarity. Proper preparation is crucial to performing at your best.

A top-tier show barn, paired with a highly skilled coach and an experienced road manager, is invaluable to your success. Your road manager will ensure that the daily schedules and estimated class times are posted the night before, allowing you to prepare accordingly. Your coach will always take the time to walk the course with you, providing essential insights and confirming your order of go.

In many lower-level jumper classes, you may find yourself competing against 35 to 50 or more riders. Regardless of the competition size, every serious rider understands the importance of proper preparation. This includes eating a well-balanced dinner and getting enough rest the night before—both critical for maintaining peak performance.

Each day at the show, you must set clear goals for yourself. The number one rule: strive to be the best version of yourself. The key to success in the ring isn't just physical ability; it's mental sharpness. A great rider is a *Thinking Rider*, not just a reactive or overly physical one. Work closely with your coach to set strategic objectives for each show. Your first year will be a significant learning experience—expect challenges, but also embrace them as opportunities to grow.

To improve as a competitor, observation is just as important as practice. Watch experienced riders perform, analyze their rounds, and record videos of different jumper and equitation rounds for later review. Listen to your coach, follow your game plan, and take mental notes on what works and what doesn't. When walking the course with your coach, don't just follow along—actively listen, process the information, and ask questions to clarify any uncertainties.

Every serious rider, whether junior or amateur, should make time to observe classes in the Medal/Equitation and Jumper rings. Simply watching isn't enough—*look and see.* Analyze each round with a critical eye. Identify what went right or wrong for each horse and rider pair, then discuss your observations with your coach and peers. Evaluate different situations and ask yourself how you would handle them. This kind of active learning will sharpen your ability to make split-second decisions in the ring.

Preparation before your ride is just as important as the competition itself. Always be on your horse at least 30 minutes before your scheduled class. Your flat warm-up should be approached with the same focus and discipline as a lesson with your coach. The best coaches arrive at the warm-up ring about 7-10 horses before your turn, ensuring you have a solid 20 minutes to fine-tune your ride before heading into the ring.

As you warm up, stay methodical and composed. You don't need to jump an excessive number of fences—five or six quality jumps are usually enough. Before warming up, spend time at the back gate observing the course and watching other riders. Your mind will be racing with anticipation, so maintaining composure and sticking to your game plan is crucial. Your coach may adjust small details based on what they observe, so stay flexible but focused.

The purpose of your warm-up isn't just to clear jumps—it's to establish the right *rhythm, feel, and motion* between you and your horse. Your timing at the canter and gallop must be in sync so that when you enter the ring, you and your horse move as one. Every step, every transition, every jump should feel natural and fluid. With the right preparation, a clear mindset, and a structured approach, you set yourself up for success in the show ring.

Falling Off in Any Class Means Automatic Elimination

Let's talk about falling off! It happens to all of us—because staying on is part of learning how to ride. The truth is, we create about 90% of our own falls. If you ever feel yourself losing balance and know you won't be able to recover, take control of the situation. Use one or both hands to push yourself away from the horse. As you hit the ground, focus on breaking your fall by rolling onto your hip and seat bone to minimize impact.

If you're not hurt, you'll know right away. Get up, dust yourself off, and walk calmly toward your horse. Most horses—99% of them—will stop immediately, standing there puzzled and watching you. Someone will be there to give you a leg-up, so get back on.

Falling off can rattle you, and that's okay. You might feel embarrassed, nervous, or even a little shaken—that's completely normal. But remember, you're an equestrian athlete. If you're physically and mentally fine, avoid the unnecessary drama. Don't just lay there. You don't need sympathy, and you certainly don't want to be pitied.

If you were competing in a class, lead your horse out of the ring on his left side and exit with composure. If you were in a lesson or warming up—whether at a show or at home—take a moment to collect yourself. Once you're ready, someone will assist you back into the saddle. Walk and trot for five minutes, then get back to your schooling or lesson.

However, if you suspect you may have injured yourself, stay on your back and wait for medical attention. A medic and your coach will assess your condition, and if you're at home, your coach will take care of you there as well.

One hard rule: Parents and spouses must stay out of the ring, whether at home or at a show. The fewer people crowding around, the better. No one needs an audience hovering over them in a moment like this. Let the trainers handle the situation immediately.

I competed at the National Horse Show in Del Mar, California, riding my wife's 4-foot working horse, *Morrocco*, in an evening class. He was a fantastic Warmblood Cross, powerful yet smooth. That same year, I had lost my lower left leg in a boat accident. Fortunately, the amputation was below the knee, which meant I still had control from the knee up.

During my round, I was coming down a line that consisted of a six-stride to a one-stride vertical-oxer combination—everything was going smoothly. But just as we landed from the vertical and approached the oxer, someone in the box seats either dropped or threw something heavy onto the cement floor. The sudden, loud noise startled *Morrocco*. In that split second between fences, he slammed to a stop. I, however, did not.

I was thrown over his head, and as I hit the ground, my left prosthetic was pulled clean off. The foot remained stuck in the stirrup, and *Morrocco*—completely unfazed—took off, galloping around the ring. I landed, momentarily sat on the ground, then hopped up on my right leg, standing there while my horse continued his victory lap—my prosthetic leg still attached to the stirrup.

The grandstands and box seats were packed. Everyone who didn't know me thought I had literally lost my leg in the accident. Gasps, shock, and sheer panic rippled through the crowd. Meanwhile, my friends, trainers, and fellow exhibitors—who knew me well—burst into laughter, realizing it was just my plastic leg making the rounds.

The announcer quickly reassured the crowd, explaining that I was perfectly fine, and that *Morrocco* was simply enjoying a solo lap with my fake leg in tow. Once the initial shock wore off, laughter and applause erupted from the stands. The spectacle had turned from horror to hilarity.

I calmly sat back down in the ring, reattached my prosthesis, and with help from the steward and ring crew, got a leg up. To show everyone I was truly fine, I cantered around the arena, then, as I made my exit, I jumped a fence and waved everyone *adoo*!

The lesson? If you're okay, get up. Shake it off. Regain your composure. A true equestrian doesn't dwell on a fall—he rides on with pride.

In any sport, mishaps happen. But as long as you and your horse are uninjured, never hold up a horse show longer than it takes to dust yourself off. Keep moving forward.

Now, let's move forward and return to Our Equestrian Center. The Horse Show has come to an end, and you, along with your fellow riders and horses, are preparing to head home. After the intensity of competition, your Horse deserves a well-earned break. Over the next two days, your Horse will have downtime to recover and reset. This period includes turnout time, allowing your Horse to move freely and relax. A thorough soap bath and rubdown will help soothe any soreness and refresh your Horse after the show. Take your Horse for a walk, let them graze, and allow them to simply be a Horse—Of-Course.

By the third day, it's time to ease back into work. A light hack, a relaxed trail ride, or a simple flat lesson with your Coach will help your Horse transition back into training without strain. On the fourth day, a dressage lesson is ideal. This structured session will reinforce rhythm, balance, and precision, helping both you and your Horse refine your skills. Remember, progress is continuous. Every ride enhances your Horse's agility, strengthens their current movements, and introduces new techniques. With consistency and dedication, you and your Horse will always be on the path to the WINNER'S CIRCLE.

Conrad Homfeld and "Gem Twist"

CHAPTER 12

'HORSE-SHOWING ON THE CIRCUIT,"

TWO OR MORE WEEKS IN A ROW.

Susie Hutchinson

You've been home for a couple of weeks, taking the time to get yourself mentally organized while settling back into your routine—whether that means returning to school or resuming work. During this period, you and your coach have discussed the upcoming Horse Shows you'll be attending, ensuring you're prepared for the events ahead.

While you're at home, if you're in school, your priorities remain clear and structured: Family comes first, followed by School, Homework, Exams, and then Training with your Horse. Maintaining this balance is crucial to your development both academically and in your equestrian pursuits.

On the logistical side, your coach or the Barn Manager will handle the administrative details, including submitting show entries, securing stabling, booking hotels, and arranging transportation. If you are a Junior, your parents will take care of the financial aspects, making sure their checkbook or credit card is ready for prepayments required for your next series of Shows.

You and your coach will also take the time to sit down and strategize, mapping out the classes you'll be competing in and defining clear objectives for each event. Throughout your first year, your focus will not only be on improving your physical skills but also on developing the ability to think critically as a rider. As you progress, your coach will determine when it's time for you to move up or transition into a different division based on your achievements and readiness.

With each Show and Class, you will continue to grow alongside your Horse, refining your equitation and competing in medal classes over fences. At the same time, you will be advancing in your jumper classes, steadily building your skills and experience. This journey is about continuous improvement, both in the saddle and in your overall approach to competition, ensuring that you and your Horse are always evolving and expanding your repertoire.

Below is a breakdown of the heights for various Equitation, Medal, and Jumper classes. These measurements are approximate and may vary within 1-2 inches:

- **.90 meters** – 3 feet
- **1 meter** – 3 feet 3 inches
- **1.10/1.15 meters** – 3 feet 6 inches and above
- **1.20 meters** – 3 feet 9 inches

- **1.30/1.35 meters** – 4 feet 3 inches and above

- **1.45 meters** – 4 feet 9 inches

- **1.50 meters** – 5 feet 3 inches

- **1.60 meters** – 5 feet 6 inches

Jump Types and Widths:

- Oxers have a set width, ranging from 3 feet to over 6 feet (Triple Bar).

- Water jumps vary in width from 6 feet to 12 feet.

- A Liverpool placed under an oxer is typically 4 feet wide.

- Oxers are generally easier for a horse to jump than a vertical, as they provide a more inviting shape with a natural bascule.

- The approach to an oxer versus a vertical is different and requires adjustments in riding technique, which will be covered in this chapter.

Riding Strategy for Open Distances and Jump-Offs

At this stage in your riding and showing career, you have likely walked multiple jumper courses with your coach, analyzed the striding, and understood how different lines and combinations ride. However, when you are faced with an open distance between obstacles—typically anything beyond seven strides—or a roll-back turn, slice, or long gallop to the final fence in a jump-off, your ability to ride off your eye becomes essential.

By now, you and your horse should have developed a strong partnership. You are familiar with your horse's natural 12-foot stride and comfortable with his 14-16-foot hand-gallop stride. When in doubt, the best approach is to ride off the seat of your pants—maintaining your forward motion, trusting your eye, and making a final stride adjustment only if absolutely necessary.

Your riding mechanics should be simple and effective:

- If your horse is bold and confident, stay upright in your three-point position, keeping your hands slightly lifted and together. Maintain a steady rhythm, ensuring that your horse remains balanced on his haunches so he can push off powerfully, even if the distance to the final fence is slightly long.

- If your horse is more cautious, use both natural and artificial aids to collect him. Three strides before takeoff, apply a half-halt along with your "whoa" voice cue to encourage an additional stride, making the approach more comfortable for your horse.

Your ability to read distances and make these adjustments comes from consistent practice. Pole exercises at home are key—working over small jumps, verticals, and square oxers sharpens your eye and refines your timing. A standard exercise includes setting two obstacles 96 feet apart and practicing different stride options to build adjustability and confidence.

In competition, once you and your horse clear the final fence, stay in half-seat position and gallop efficiently through the timers, ensuring you complete the course with speed and control.

Therefore, when riding between the designated distances, you will follow a structured approach. The standard distance will require seven strides, but you will also practice variations by adjusting to either eight or six strides. After each adjustment, you must focus on landing over the first fence—whether it's an oxer or a vertical. If the oxer comes first, you are covering more ground over the jump, meaning you must initiate either a shortening or lengthening of your horse's stride upon landing. This decision depends on the next element in the course. You will either land and gallop forward to maintain momentum or land and shorten your stride to prepare for the next fence.

For consistency, you should practice a combination of seven-, eight-, and six-stride approaches over a six-foot distance. At the end of the ring, you and your horse will execute a roll-back turn, ensuring a lead change—ideally, a flying lead change—to maintain balance and rhythm. You will repeat this exercise in various stride patterns, alternating sequences such as 7-6-8, then 8-6-7, followed by 6-8-7. Keep the two fences small at this stage to focus on precision and control rather than height.

By this point, you should have developed a sharp eye for distances, and with continued practice, both you and your horse will move fluidly through these exercises. As your feel for your horse improves and your horse's trust in you deepens, these adjustments will become second nature. Remember the key principle from an earlier chapter: always count your strides out loud. This habit not only reinforces rhythm and control but also builds confidence in your ability to measure distances accurately.

As a junior rider, you will compete in numerous equitation classes, and working with top course designers will prepare you for the transition into both primary and secondary jumper divisions. Every round you ride will require equitation fundamentals combined with quick thinking, as course designers will continuously test your adaptability. Your competition will be strong, and your precision should become second nature. Keep in mind that every ride is a test—your goal is to refine your technique, make adjustments instinctively, and sharpen your competitive edge.

Many of today's top riders, who began their careers in the Jumpers as junior riders, dedicated countless hours in the saddle refining their technical flatwork—both with and without stirrups. They weren't just talented; they had strong foundations built on discipline and repetition. They also had exceptional coaches guiding them, individuals who themselves had been successful junior riders, never stopped learning, and eventually reached the pinnacle of international competition.

If you have the means to compete in this demanding and costly sport, you need three things: a top-tier coach, a highly capable horse, and most importantly—you, the rider, with relentless commitment, courage, and the willingness to push through challenges. It takes guts to compete at the highest levels, and it takes glory to sustain success. Many amateur riders have worked their way up and found success in the jumper rings and Grand Prix arenas.

One thing remains true: many hours in the saddle and world-class horses make champions.

Recommendations for Riders

If you want to develop into a top competitor, study the best. Watch and analyze videos of Grand Prix riders and Olympians. Learn from those who have mastered the sport: Susie Hutchison, McClain Ward, Ashley Bond, Hap Hansen, Joe Vargis, Conrad Homfeld. Some of these incredible riders are also personal friends—many of us grew up in the sport together.

"A Luxury Sport, A Costly Sport"

There's no denying it—show jumping and equitation are expensive. Horse shows, training, and quality horses all come at a high price. However, many elite equitation and jumper farms offer student work programs and scholarships to help dedicated riders access opportunities.

In my 59 year career, I have coached professionally, conducted clinics worldwide, and personally provided financial assistance and riding school scholarships every year. Many top farms support young riders this way, and I typically offer between 3 and 5 scholarships per year. Some cover only lessons, while others include board, training, and reduced horse show costs.

The Importance of Clinics

Every junior and amateur rider should take at least two clinics per year with national and international riders/coaches. The value of these learning experiences cannot be overstated. Throughout my career, I worked with many of the top clinicians in dressage and Grand Prix jumping, and I continue to host top equitation trainers for multi-day clinics at Equestrian Centers International.

Even if my students learn from me every day, hearing the same concepts explained differently by other professionals adds depth to their understanding. Education in this sport is never-ending.

The Reality of Commitment

Equestrian sports are expensive, but so are most competitive sports at an elite level. The difference? This sport isn't just about the athlete—it's about the partnership between horse and rider.

I was fortunate to grow up in a wealthy family, but that didn't mean I didn't work for it. I had a paper route, worked as a box boy, and later took a job in a men's clothing store stockroom—all so I could ride and train more.

If you truly want to succeed in this sport, you'll find a way. The best riders always do.

Will Simpson

CHAPTER 13

'SHOWING JUMPING AND MEDAL FINALS, GO EAST, GO WEST, GO NORTH AND GO SOUTH!'

Richard Spooner

While training at a top Equitation or Jumper Equestrian
Center as an Amateur or Junior Show Rider, you've likely
achieved solid success within your state—perhaps even
outstanding results. When your Coach determines that
you're ready, they will recommend taking the next step:
traveling to Finals, whether as an Individual competitor,
with your Jumper Team, or in your Medal Finals.

Once Finals are over and you return home, it's time to
reassess and plan your next move. Your Coach, the
Equestrian Center you represent, and your Parents or
Family will come together to determine what that next BIG
step should be. If your goal is to become a top Equitation or
Grand Prix rider, or if you're an Amateur who wants to
maintain peak performance, you must evaluate your
options carefully. These crossroads are crucial.

At this stage, you have two primary paths. You can take
a gradual approach, easing into your Grand Prix career by
choosing selective events rather than committing to every
major show. However, if your Talent, Ambition, and
Personality drive you toward the highest level of
competition, hesitation is not an option. You must be
prepared to step up and embrace the challenge.

The world of high-level Jumper classes offers numerous opportunities, but success requires a strategic plan—one that you and your Coach must develop and follow diligently. This plan will shape your trajectory in the sport.

One undeniable factor in making the leap to top-tier competition is securing the right horse. You will need a highly competitive mount, and selecting the right one is critical. Some horses are extremely careful jumpers but may lack the necessary speed. Others are quick off the ground but might occasionally knock a rail. Then, there are those rare horses that have it all: size, agility, precision, and a proven winning record. A winning record means consistently placing in the top four of their class. One of my preferred choices is a Thoroughbred/Warmblood cross—a combination that often brings together the best traits of both breeds.

Of course, all of this comes down to one essential factor: cost. The question isn't just what you can afford but, more importantly, what it takes to remain truly competitive. Balancing financial investment with competitive potential is a crucial part of your journey forward.

Gran-Prix horses come with a significant price range, starting from approximately $500,000 and reaching up to

$10,000,000 with plenty of options in between. The ideal scenario for serious competitors would be owning two horses—one specifically for speed classes, excelling in 4'6" to 4'9" jumps with precision and agility, and a dedicated Gran-Prix horse capable of tackling heights from 4'9" to 5'6", with most top courses set around 5'3".

Participating in horse shows becomes increasingly expensive due to nomination fees, class entry fees, and various additional costs that accumulate over time. However, one of the most invaluable investments you can make is hiring a top-tier groom who genuinely cares for your horses. A skilled groom is worth their weight in gold, ensuring your horses are in peak condition and anticipating your needs without any unexpected surprises. They are as knowledgeable about your classes as you and your coach, making them an essential part of a successful team.

The Gran-Prix World of Today and Tomorrow

If these costs and commitments do not align with your personal, business, or financial situation—or if the sheer amount of time required for training, travel, and living out of suitcases in hotels, motels, or other temporary accommodations is not feasible—there are still plenty of options available.

In previous chapters, I have outlined various competitive circuits that allow riders to continue pursuing their passion without committing to the national and international Gran-Prix circuits, where million-dollar competitions dominate. County and state-level horse shows still offer excellent opportunities to compete in Mini-Prix events, speed classes, and Gran-Prix competitions ranging from $500 to $25,000 in prize money. You do not need to be part of the elite million-dollar circuit to experience high-level competition and achieve your goals.

Beyond financial considerations, reducing road expenses can make competing more manageable. One of the best investments for riders looking to maintain independence and control over their schedule is purchasing a personal 2-3 horse slant trailer with a ramp and dressing room. Modern models come equipped with essential amenities such as a bathroom, sink, refrigerator, stove, and even sleeping quarters, making travel much more convenient. Additionally, a well-equipped 1 to 1.5-ton, four-door truck is necessary for safe and efficient transportation.

However, these logistical choices should always be discussed with your coach and road manager. In many cases, the head coach is already traveling with other riders on the high-level "A" to Triple-A (3-Star) circuits, making advance planning crucial. At the end of each year, you must determine and commit to your equestrian show jumping budget. No well-established equitation or jumper farm—nor its staff—appreciates last-minute surprises when it comes to financial and logistical commitments.

Throughout my book, I chose not to discuss riding in the Hunters division. When you first begin competing, you will primarily enter smaller classes, which may be judged either on your performance as a rider or on your horse's way of going.

The Hunters are often considered a foundational aspect of learning to ride, but in my experience, they are heavily influenced by politics. Over the course of your career, you will likely own between three and five solid show horses. If you compete at the county and state levels, your coach will eventually help you find a quality equitation-jumper, typically priced between $450,000 and $125,000.

In the end, always strive to give your best effort. As an athlete and a rising equestrian star, it is essential to stay dedicated. Communicate effectively, embrace both the successes and the setbacks, and remain committed to your goals. With persistence and determination, your hard work and dreams will become reality.

Joe Fargi

CONCLUSION

As this book comes to a close, we stand at a pivotal moment—the point where each rider must reflect on the lessons learned and the skills developed, yet know that their journey is far from over. The sport of equitation, like all endeavors, is a constant evolution, where mastery is only ever a fleeting moment before new challenges arise. This is the beauty of the equestrian path: the unending pursuit of excellence, the bond between horse and rider, and the daily commitment to growth.

Whether you're a young rider just beginning to dream of Olympic glory or an experienced equestrian refining your technique, remember this: the road ahead is filled with opportunities for development. It's not just about winning ribbons or competing at the highest levels—though those milestones are significant—it's about fostering a relationship with your horse, nurturing your instincts, and continually expanding your knowledge.

Equestrian sports are more than just a physical challenge; they are a mental and emotional journey that require dedication, resilience, and heart. Each lesson, each ride, each competition adds another layer to your growth—not just as a rider, but as a person. The same discipline, focus, and patience that serve you in the arena will shape your character in every aspect of life.

In closing, I encourage you to stay true to the principles that have guided the greatest equestrians before you: commitment, respect, and a relentless pursuit of improvement. Embrace the ups and downs with grace, learn from every experience, and above all, never stop seeking knowledge. Because the true journey of an equestrian isn't about reaching a final destination, but about enjoying the ride—every twist, turn, and jump along the way.

Thank you for trusting me to be a part of your equestrian journey. I look forward to hearing where it takes you. Keep riding, keep learning, and keep growing.

"A STORY FROM THE HEART"
Equestrian Centers International

Almost 20 years ago, I came to Palm Springs (the desert), hitchhiking! Yes, this is a very true story. All of my life, I was very blessed to have a silver spoon upbringing (or maybe not!). When I reached my thirties, I thought I had everything any man could want. I had a beautiful home in Rancho Santa Fe, I had my horses, I had money, I was Vice President of Cintas Development, and plenty of friends to party with.

What I did not have was self-respect. I had not taken the time to evaluate my life and set a straight and narrow path for my future. The worst was that I was burning the candle at both ends, and not taking other people's feelings to heart.

So, one day, I went to my office and found out that I had no job, no family, no house, no car, and two hundred dollars to my name. Yes! At that moment, my world had fallen apart. My father and the board totally exiled me.

By this time, I had already had my leg accident and 36 surgeries trying to save my leg, and still, I had no idea how long I would be able to keep it.

I picked myself up, a suitcase in hand, two hundred dollars in my pocket, and I hitchhiked to Palm Springs. I thought the best thing to do was to get as far away as I could and start a new life.

When I arrived in the desert, I rented an efficiency apartment by the week. My mother, who had sided with me, bought me an orange (yes, orange) golf cart to go back and forth to the market. This was a big help because I was suffering from the disease "osteomyelitis," and there were times when I could not even walk without the assistance of crutches or a wheelchair.

I advertised in the Desert Sun (local rag), "Freelance Equestrian Instructor Available," teaching hunters, jumpers, hunt seat equitation! The number I left was a friend's telephone message machine!

By this time, I had been a professional for 12 years, I had a very well-respected name in San Diego, and I had my AHSA judges card. Within two days, I received phone calls from local equestrians that were seeking instruction. A month later, I had a student body of 10 riders. I needed to buy a vehicle to get from one end of the Coachella Valley to the other, but I did not have the cash to do so! My friends had gotten a little tired of driving me around, and after all, the golf cart could not go down the freeway.

I met a wonderful older lady who had advertised her 1968 gold Cadillac for sale. Her husband had just passed away. I met with Mrs. Cohen at her trailer park where she lived and explained to her that I had no money, but that I could give her a down payment and pay for the vehicle over the next year. She wanted two thousand dollars for it. I gave her two hundred dollars down and told her I would pay her two hundred dollars every month for the next nine months.

Now I had transportation, and because of this wonderful woman believing in me, in two months, I had 20 students and I was head trainer at Patti Aiken's place in Bermuda Dunes. Mrs. Cohen soon passed away, and this wonderful individual left me the gold Cadillac in her will, free and clear.

Soon afterward, Vandenberg Stables was looking for a resident trainer. I met with Mr. Bob Vandenberg and took over as their head hunter-jumper trainer. This was in 1982. That's when I met many of my students that I still instruct today. This is when Melanie Calender started to ride with me.

When I moved to Vandenberg Stables, he had approximately 18 horses stabled there. Within 9 months, Equestrian Centers Intl. (then it was called Palm Springs Equestrian Center) had 36 students and twenty-two additional horses in training. My life had begun to turn around.

I traded in the (funky) gold Cadillac from Mrs. Cohen and got myself a Chevrolet "Blazer," something that matched my career and could pull a horse trailer.

Within a two-and-a-half-year period, my father had made contact with me again and had found out that I was on the road to success, and that I had done it on my own. We started the road back to becoming a father-and-son relationship. Within the next year, I was able to buy a house in Palm Springs on San Lucas.

The road to my second life was coming together.

Soon after, I met my wife-to-be, Kathy Cintas. She started riding with me when she was in the desert taking care of her business for Hot Dog on a Stick as Chief Financial Officer. Within two years, Kathy and I would be married, and soon after, be blessed with three great children: Adam, and the twins, Ashley and Alysha.

A new life begins! In 1982, Joseph Wambaugh (and wife Dee) decided to sponsor me and bought me a Grand Prix horse from Europe. "Satarin," a big 17.2-hand Holsteiner (grey gelding), with a good group of students and horses, along with my jumper, we were able to compete very successfully on the "A" circuit again.

Just as things were looking up, I was showing a green horse at Indio (during the days of the Indio Date Festival). The young horse spooked, tripped, and fell down, smashing my left leg. At that time, the osteomyelitis was very bad (I had to inject myself through a catheter four times a day in my chest), and that was all it took for me to lose my leg.

I was rushed to Sharp Memorial in San Diego. I had called ahead and told Doctor Forney what had happened, and that I wanted this leg off once and for all. That evening, my leg was amputated. I woke up the next morning to a new man—no pain, no more injections, no more drugs.

I had suffered for 15 years with this. When I saw my doctor the next day, I said, "When will I be able to ride again?" He said, "2-3 months." I said, "I have a horse show in three weeks," and through the will of God, I was showing and jumping three weeks later. So back to business!

My business was doing very well, and it was time to either buy or build a place in the valley. Joseph Wambaugh suggested that we find out if Mr. Vandenberg wanted to sell his place. The answer was yes, he wanted $900,000 for 7 acres in Cathedral City (this was in 1982). Michael and Joe discussed it, and after reviewing the capabilities of this stable and future earnings, together they decided to offer Mr. Vandenberg $750,000 cash. Although in those years this was a very generous offer, Mr. Vandenberg turned it down. I discussed this with Joe, and they were not willing together to make a counteroffer. At this time, I knew that it was time to take the next step and build my own place. I discussed this with my future wife-to-be, and she encouraged me to move forward.

We shopped around in various communities of the desert, and the best place to build was Rancho Mirage. We found the first 5 acres where the main complex is built in late 1982. The land was under the sphere of influence of Rancho Mirage but still in the county of Riverside.

I went back to Mr. Vandenberg and told him that I would be building my own place. He looked at me and said, "You have 30 days to vacate." I told him that there was no way I could have a place built in that time, but his mind was made up.

I called my father and asked him for some help with a down payment that would assure me of acquiring the land, and he willingly obliged.

On acquiring the first five acres, the first thing we did on this deep desert sand lot was to grade an area so that we could put up a temporary riding ring and corrals. Within two weeks, we moved over 30 clients and horses.

The clients were wonderful about working in temporary facilities, temporary bathrooms (just plain temporary everything) while we built Equestrian Centers Intl.

By June of 1984, the superstructure was up, and the stalls were complete surrounding the indoor arena. At last, we were able to move the clients and horses to our new facility. That same year, Kathy and I were married.

Business continued to grow, and by the following year, we had our landscaping done and our outside arenas, jumping chute, and turn-outs. By this time, we were doing the Arizona Circuit, Calgary, Canada, and the Pony Finals in Culpeper, Virginia.

In 1986, my son Adam was born, the first happiest day of my life. Eleven months later, his twin sisters (Ashley and Alysha) were born, my second happiest moment in my life. All I could think was how wonderful and complete my life really was.

We continued to grow by leaps and bounds. We were off to Europe buying new prospects for our clientele and continuing to win on the "A" circuit.

It was time to bring another top professional on board, and in 1988, David Chartrand arrived from New York to work alongside me. There have been many trainers who have come and gone since then.

Because of all the good friends, family, and the faith I have in humanity, I look back at the first half of my life and thank God for every day I have been able to live it.

"Never say never." We all have the same opportunities in life to succeed! We can turn any negative into a positive, be honest to ourselves, and love all mankind!

"THE BEGINNING, THE MIDDLE & THE END"
Coach Michael

My Life has always been blessed, even at times when things looked bleak, right over the Mountain was The Glowing Sun and you could see forever! Some of my biggest blunders in life were my most wonderful awakenings. Hit by a neighbor's car, because I was running across the street to Mrs. George's House to get candy, I learned it was ok to run, but first look and see where you are going! I was 9 years old.

When I was 21 years old, on Our Fathers "APOLLO" maiden voyage, I was Selfish and Self-Centered and thought I was the best and took everything for granted.

I Had that disease 'ARROGANCE' & SELF-RIGHTGEOUS.

When we were 20 miles outside the Port of Salinas, Ecuador, I stepped into a towline, and there I went upside down through the porthole into the Pacific Ocean

Until the tow line became taunt and ripped my left lower leg off except for the main artery. I found myself and that I was just another spoiled punk and nothing special.

That was the day that my life went before me, and I should have been dead. It was a good lesson for me to go through. In those 90 seconds in the Pacific Ocean, I prayed to God, please let me live and raise a family and go back to what I was the best at, "HORSES" I realized within those 90 seconds, I was just another human-being blessed with being a excellent rider, trainer, coach and if they could save my leg I promised God that I would get this Very Big Chip off of my shoulder and try to become a whole and real person, this accident is what saved my life. The wake-up call changed me for life. From that moment on I became a giver and not a taker, and No-One owed me anything, but I surely owed so much to my family, my friends, my students, the Human Race. Humility has stayed with me ever since.

I kept my leg for 15 years with the disease osteomyelitis and always in terrible pain. But it made me appreciate life to the fullest, and how to love and respect everyone around me, and how to Slow Down and appreciate all the blessings I had.

Believe me, I became a softer, kinder, sensitive rider, teacher, coach and through all of this 'A REAL PERSON'

The biggest Test of all was right around the corner, 15 years later, when a young horse without a rider ran at full speed into my young horse and knocked us over at the warm-up ring at Empire Polo, The Desert Circuit.

My horse fell right on top of me and particularly on my Osteo leg. I had already had 36 operations to save the leg, but I had grown up and reality set in, I told my wife Kathy, the time had come. I had my leg amputated. I had given it all, but the time was right, another blessing in disguise. I had my left lower leg amputated and said to myself "SELF" you have a Horse Show in 6 weeks, you pick yourself up when your stump heals, put your pipe leg on, and put your straps around your waist and go back to what you do best. Horses, students, farm, family

And never look back.

Believe it or not, I became even a better rider and road for the next 30 years. My students were winners, my family knew my personality and I practiced very hard, that I never had a limp.

The Beginning the Middle and the End. 56 years of being a professional trainer, teacher, mentor and the honor of being an Olympic Coach. Always owning my own farms with my family, making wonderful Equitation riders from the time they were 6-7 years old and most stayed training with me until they went off to college. Traveled around the

World as A Coach & Clinician, the Olympic Games, Pan-Am's, World Cups, Nation Cups.

I may not look old, nor do I act old (I think) But my body and God was telling me to hang up the boots and you will be able to stay around awhile longer. I canceled Escrow on the New Farm and for whatever time I have left finish writing my 3 books. "Learning to Ride-RIGHT" , Become An Equitation Rider with feel and sensitivity , "THE MAKING OF AN EQUITATION RIDER TODAY" not a mannequin. And the 3rd Book "The Cintas Stigma"

I just want to say I Thank You All, I Love You All, and to God, thanks for all the Wake-Up Calls!

Coach Michael

Ian Millar of Canada competes in the Pan American Games. (Nathan Denette/CP)

George Morris Clinic Given in 2012 at Equestrian Centers International - Clinic Dinner Party At Coach Michael's House

www.ingramcontent.com/pod-product-compliance
Lightning Source LLC
Chambersburg PA
CBHW051209120626
46547CB00013B/1269